MY FIRST
SCIENCE
EXPERIMENTS
BOOK

This book belongs to

....

Note to Parents

Welcome to *My First Science Experiments Book!*

The activities in this book are intended to provide your child with engaging, hands-on experiments that build science knowledge and understanding. They are divided into four groups: chemistry and physics, biology, Earth science, and technology. Most of the equipment and materials required can be found around the home or at regular stores.

Here are some tips to help ensure that your child gets the most from this book.

★ Read through an experiment before beginning to ensure your child has the materials needed and is able to complete it safely. Messy experiments are best done on wipe-clean surfaces or outside.

★ Encourage your child to enjoy getting messy and experimenting. As long as your child remains safe, allow him or her to modify the experiments to figure out what happens if one or another variable is changed.

★ Help your child to think about the science behind the experiment. For example, ask, "Why do you think we need to use hot water?" After your child completes an experiment, ask him or her to explain what happened to identify any gaps in his or her understanding.

★ Create an environment where curiosity is valued. If you don't have an answer to one of your child's science questions, encourage him or her research the answer online or in a library book.

★ If an experiment doesn't work, encourage your child to look back at the steps to identify any mistakes and to try again.

We wish your child hours of fun and learning with these experiments!

Scholastic Early Learning

Picture credits: All photos on section openers and *It's STEM!* pages courtesy of **Shutterstock**, unless noted as follows: **FotograFFF_Shutterstock.com:** 88cl (hovercraft); **Jo Hunter_Shutterstock.com:** 88tl (hovercraft); **muroPhotographer_shutterstock.com:** 88tr (hovercraft); **tartanparty_ Shutterstock.com:** 80bl (catapult ride); **vsop_Shutterstock.com:** 7tr (spring); **Zaferkizilkaya_Shutterstock.com:** 28bl (diver).

With thanks to **William Reavell** for the experiment photography. Thanks also to our wonderful models: Bethany, Emilee, George, Harris, Hyder, Issy, Riley, and Ruby.

Contents

How to Use **This Book**

The experiments in this book can be done in any order you want. Look through the book and choose which one you'd like to do. This page will show you how to get the most out of the experiment.

Materials list
Use this list to prepare everything you need.

Experiment title

The science bit
This paragraph tells you about the science behind the experiment. You can find the meanings of the bold words in the glossary.

Eroding Rocks

Rocks and mountains may seem like they'll last forever, but over many years, wind and water break down the most solid rock. This process is called **erosion**.

YOU WILL NEED:
• sand
• water
• a waterproof tray
• a hair dryer
• a small watering can

Steps
Read through all the steps before you start. Then follow them in order.

1
Use sand and a little water to make four "rocks," each the size of a tennis ball. Put the rocks to one side.

2
Put two rocks in a tray. One is your control. The other is the experimental rock.

3
Use the hair dryer to blast the experimental rock with "wind" for a few minutes.

4
Use the watering can to simulate rain falling on another rock.

WARNING!
TO AVOID AN ELECTRIC SHOCK, DO NOT GET WATER NEAR THE HAIR DRYER.

5
Use the hair dryer and then the watering can on a third rock to simulate a storm.

62

Safety warning
Carefully read and follow any safety warnings.

IT'S MONUMENTAL!

AMAZING NATURAL ROCK FORMATIONS DEVELOP WHEN SOME ROCKS ERODE FASTER THAN OTHERS.

RIVER EROSION

You could also try using sand and water to create a model mountain. Trickle water down its side to see how rivers create canyons and valleys.

63

Stickers
There are four sheets of fun stickers at the back of the book.

QR code
Scan the QR code for a step-by-step instruction video.

Scan the **QR code** for step-by-step instructions!

Take it further
You'll find suggestions for fun ways to extend or vary the experiment here.

Chemistry and Physics

Chemistry is the branch of science that investigates substances, or **chemicals**, and the way they interact with one another. Scientists who work in this area are called **chemists**.

Physics is the branch of science that studies physical processes. **Physicists** investigate such things as matter, energy, force, mechanics, sound, light, and heat.

Growing Crystals

Crystals form when molecules join together in a regularly repeating pattern. Many crystals form naturally in nature, but you can make your own crystals, too.

1 Ask an adult to measure the hot water into the large measuring cup. Add several drops of food coloring and stir.

WARNING!
DO NOT DRINK THE SALT WATER OR EAT EPSOM SALTS. THEY MAY CAUSE AN UPSET STOMACH.

4 Use thread to hang the fuzzy shape from a pencil.

2 Add the Epsom salts to the water, and stir until they are completely dissolved. Then pour the liquid into the jar.

5 Hang the shape in the jar so it is submerged. Place the jar in the refrigerator overnight.

3 Twist the pipe cleaner around a cookie cutter to make a shape.

WATCH IT SPARKLE!

TAKE IT FURTHER

Try bending pipe cleaners into other shapes or even your name to make delicate crystal decorations. Be sure to keep them away from young children and pets.

Candy Colors

The amount of a substance in a mixture is called its **concentration**. Chemicals move from areas of higher concentration to areas of lower concentration. When you add water to sugarcoated candies, the colored sugar dissolves in the water and moves from the highly concentrated candy to the lesser concentrated water.

1 Arrange the candies in a ring around the edge of the plate. Don't put candies of the same color beside one another.

2 Ask an adult to help you pour in warm water until it just covers the plate and touches the candies. Watch closely!

ARRANGE THE CANDIES IN DIFFERENT PATTERNS. YOU COULD TRY LIMITING THE NUMBER OF COLORS YOU USE OR MAKING A RING WITHIN A RING.

Scan the **QR code** for step-by-step instructions!

MAKE FUN SHAPES!

THE COLORS DON'T MIX BECAUSE THE CONCENTRATION OF SUGAR IS THE SAME IN EACH ONE.

TIME CHECK

How quickly does it take for the colors to meet in the center of the plate? First, time the experiment using cold water, and then time it again using hot water (with an adult's help). Which way works faster?

11

Homemade Ice Cream

Adding salt to ice lowers its **freezing point**. This causes the ice in the outer bag to absorb heat from the ice-cream mixture in the inner bag. As it melts, the ice-cream mixture freezes.

YOU WILL NEED:
- 1 cup half-and-half
- 2 tbsp white sugar
- ½ tsp vanilla extract
- 1 small zipper bag
- 1 large zipper bag
- 3 cups ice
- ⅓ cup salt
- a dish towel
- warm gloves

1 Pour the half-and-half, sugar, and vanilla into the small zipper bag.

2 Seal the bag tightly. Shake it to mix the ingredients.

3 Open the bag again and carefully squeeze out the air. Zip it tightly closed.

4 Place the ice and salt inside the large zipper bag, and then place the sealed small bag inside it.

5 Squeeze out the air and close the large zipper bag tightly.

6 Wrap the large bag in a dish towel. Put on your gloves and shake the bag for five minutes, or until the mixture forms the texture of ice cream.

7 Unwrap the dish towel and unzip the large bag. Remove the small bag and rinse off the salty water.

THIS IS YUMMY!

YOU COULD ALSO TRY ...

... adding different flavors to your ice cream. You might like to add chocolate chips or use peppermint extract instead of vanilla. You could also scatter colorful sprinkles on top.

It's STEM!

Diamond is the strongest known material. Tiny laboratory-grown diamond **crystals** are used on polishing tools and drills to make them extra tough.

Quartz **crystals** are used in watch batteries. An electric current causes the crystal to vibrate at a regular pace. This ensures the watch keeps accurate time.

Color-coated candies are all the same color until the outer layer is added. This machine is adding yellow coloring as candies turn in a drum.

Fabric manufacturers add chemical **fixatives** to **dyed material**. If they didn't do this, the color would run when the fabric was washed in the same way that the color runs from candies in water.

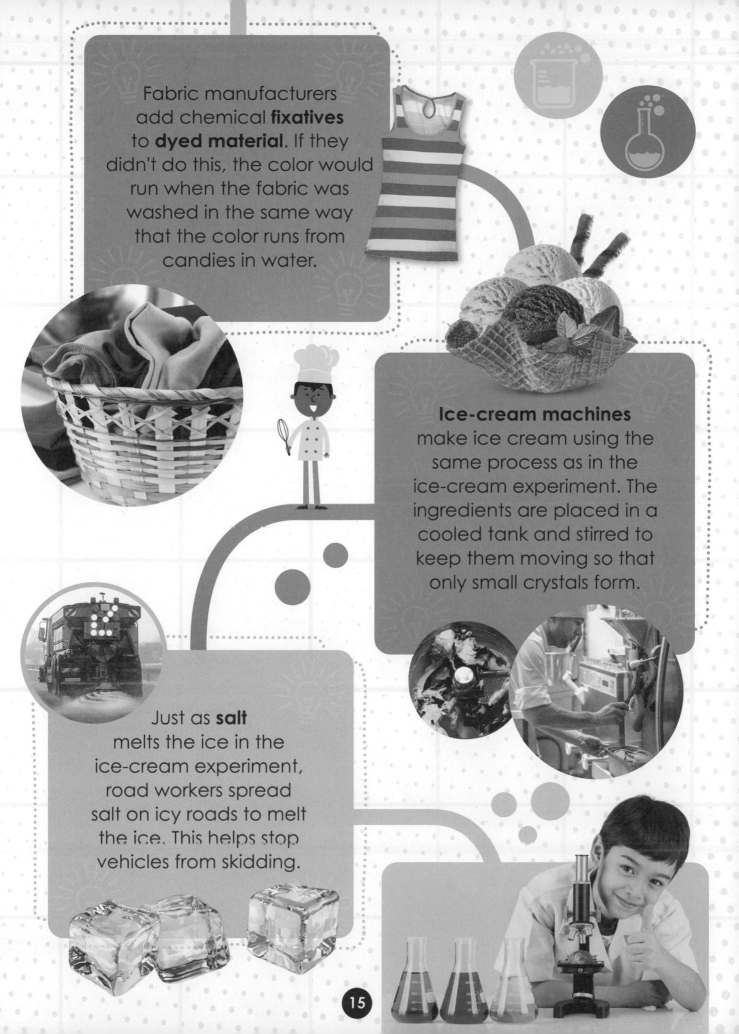

Ice-cream machines make ice cream using the same process as in the ice-cream experiment. The ingredients are placed in a cooled tank and stirred to keep them moving so that only small crystals form.

Just as **salt** melts the ice in the ice-cream experiment, road workers spread salt on icy roads to melt the ice. This helps stop vehicles from skidding.

Self-Inflating Balloon

How can you inflate a balloon without blowing into it or using helium? You can use chemistry! When baking soda and vinegar combine, they create a gas called **carbon dioxide**, which is light and rises up into the balloon. This is a **chemical reaction** in action!

1 Place the funnel in the top of the bottle and pour in the vinegar.

2 Clean and dry the funnel. Then carefully wrap the end of the balloon around the narrow end of the funnel. Holding them together, slowly tip the baking soda into the balloon.

3 With an adult's help, wrap the end of the balloon over the mouth of the bottle. Make sure the top of the balloon hangs down so that the baking soda doesn't fall into the bottle.

4 Lift the balloon and shake it gently so the baking soda pours into the bottle. Hold the bottom of the balloon as the baking soda and vinegar react.

LOSE THE BALLOON

You can do a simple version of this experiment. Place the bottle on a tray or in a sink, and pour the baking soda directly into the vinegar. What happens?

TEST AND TRY

Experiment with the quantities. If you add a little more baking soda or vinegar, will the balloon grow bigger?

WATCH IT INFLATE!

FOAM FUN

Place the bottle on a tray or in a sink. Add a squirt of dish soap and a few drops of food coloring to the vinegar. Then pour the baking soda directly into the bottle.

Scan the **QR code** for step-by-step instructions!

Glitter Slime

The glue in slime is a **polymer**, a material made of long, thin molecules. When you add the contact-lens solution, the chains link up, creating a thick slime.

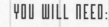
1

Pour the glue into a mixing bowl. Stir in the baking soda.

2

Pour the contact-lens solution into the mixture.

3

Stir in the contact-lens solution.

4

Add the paint and the glitter.

5

Keep stirring as the mixture slowly turns into slime. When the slime comes away cleanly from the sides of the bowl, leave it to rest for two minutes. Then have fun!

STREEEEEEETCH IT!

BLOW IT UP!

SQUEEZE IT!

Non-Newtonian Goo

Solid materials keep their shape. Liquid materials can flow or be poured. A **non-Newtonian fluid** is an unusual substance that can either be solid or liquid depending on the pressure put on it. When you squeeze it, the particles lock together and react like a solid, but when you let it go, the particles flow through your fingers like a liquid!

YOU WILL NEED:

- 2 cups cornstarch
- a mixing bowl
- 1 tsp washable acrylic paint
- a wooden spoon
- 1–2 cups water

1 Tip the cornstarch into the bowl.

2 Add a teaspoon of paint to 1 cup of water and stir.

3 Slowly pour the colored water into the cornstarch and stir them together.

4 When the mixture becomes too stiff to stir, use your hands to knead it together.

5 Continue adding water a little at a time until the mixture is gloopy but not too runny. It should be a thick liquid that hardens when you press on it. (If you add too much water, just add a little more cornstarch.)

POUR IT!
Pour it into your hand. Then squeeze the mixture that's in your palm. What happens when you let go?

NOTE!
THIS EXPERIMENT CAN GET MESSY. WEAR AN APRON, AND USE A COVERED WORK SURFACE OR AN OUTSIDE SPACE.

TRY THESE TESTS!

RIP IT!
Quickly drag your fingers through the goo. Can you rip it? How far can you get?

SLAP IT!
Slap the goo with your hand. Does it splash or feel solid?

21

It's STEM!

The borate ions in the contact-lens solution link up the long-chain **molecules** in the glue, making a thick slime. However, these links are weak. They easily break and reform. This is why slime is moldable.

Slime is **viscous**, which means it is thick and pours slowly. It gets less viscous and easier to stretch or pour when it is warm.

When baking soda reacts with the acid in milk, it gives off bubbles of **carbon-dioxide** gas. This is what makes cake mixtures rise to become light, airy cakes.

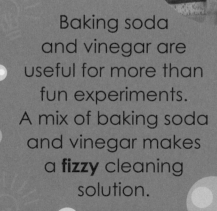

Baking soda and vinegar are useful for more than fun experiments. A mix of baking soda and vinegar makes a **fizzy** cleaning solution.

Non-Newtonian goo gets more viscous, or thick, under pressure. That's why it feels solid when you press it and returns to a liquid when you let it go.

Engineers have developed a **non-Newtonian fluid** to use in body armor. The fluid is light and flexible in normal conditions but becomes a solid shield if hit hard.

Fruit-salad recipes often include **lemon juice**. The acid in the lemon juice stops the apple turning brown.

Disco Milk

The molecules at the surface of a liquid pull on one another more strongly than the molecules below. This creates a film-like layer called **surface tension**. In this experiment, the food coloring sits on the surface, but then the dish soap breaks the surface tension, causing all the molecules to move about.

Scan the **QR code** for step-by-step instructions!

1

Pour milk into the plate until the base is covered. Then add a few drops of each food coloring to the milk. Space out the colors, but keep them near the center of the plate.

2

Add a small drop of dish soap to one end of the cotton swab.

BE CAREFUL!
FOOD COLORING CAN STAIN.

3

Dip the cotton swab into the center of the milk and in a few other places.

YOU WILL NEED:
- milk
- a flat white plate
- 3 different food colorings
- dish soap
- a cotton swab

SEE THE COLORS SWIRL!

Soap-Powered Boat

Surface tension holds a cardboard boat in place on water. When you add dish soap, it breaks the water's surface tension. The boat is pulled away from the water with lower surface tension to the parts that still have higher tension.

1 Cut a simple boat shape from the cardboard. Then carefully cut a notch in the back of the boat. You can copy the shape of this one.

THERE IT GOES!

2 Place the boat gently on the water.

3 Using a toothpick, add a drop of dish soap to the inside the notch.

Brown Apples

When an apple is cut, chemicals inside it react with oxygen in the air. This is called **oxidization**. It turns the apple brown. Acids can stop oxidization. Lemon juice is an acid. So is vinegar, but it is not as strong as lemon juice. Milk is a weak acid. Water is not acidic, but it will keep some oxygen away from the apple.

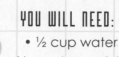

1 Pour the water, lemon juice, milk, and vinegar into separate cups.

2 Cut labels out of the paper. Label each cup with the liquid inside.

3 Cut the apple into 5 wedges. Keep one wedge aside, and place one wedge in each cup, ensuring it is covered in liquid. Leave to soak for 5 minutes.

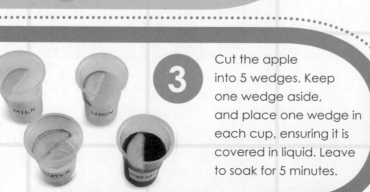

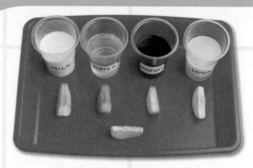

4 Remove the wedges from the liquids and place them on a tray. Keep the labels with them so they don't get mixed up. Place the wedge that you set aside on the tray as well. It is your control. Leave for 2 hours.

OBSERVE YOUR RESULTS!

OBSERVE

Which piece of apple turned the brownest?

Which piece turned the least brown?

Why do you think you got this result?

What other liquids could you try?

Biology

Biology is the branch of science that involves studying living things, such as plants, animals, and fungi. There are many types of **biologists**, such as **marine biologists** and **microbiologists**.

Fingerprint Spy

Fingerprints are the ridges of skin on the tips of your fingers. No two people have exactly the same pattern of whorls, loops, and arches on their fingertips, not even identical twins. This means detectives can analyze fingerprints to identify people.

YOU WILL NEED:
- modeling clay
- a flashlight
- a magnifying glass
- friends or family members
- a stamp pad
- a sheet of paper
- a pencil or pen

1 Ask your family or friends to choose one person to leave a thumbprint in modeling clay. Don't let them tell you "who done it."

2 Shine the flashlight at the clay on an angle to help you see the print more clearly. The magnifying glass might also help.

3 Ask each of your family or friends to press a thumb into the stamp pad and then onto the sheet of paper to leave a print. Ask them to write their names below their prints.

4 Compare the print in the clay to your sheet of different people's prints. Can you crack the case of who left the print behind?

Ben Ella ?ah Ava R?

HOW ARE THE PRINTS DIFFERENT? ANALYZE THEM!

SOME POLICE NOW USE MOBILE FINGERPRINT SCANNERS TO INSTANTLY IDENTIFY PEOPLE.

Germs Everywhere

Germs are tiny **microorganisms** that can make people sick. If a sick person sneezes or coughs without covering up, they can spread germs. They can also spread germs by touching things. By using glitter to represent germs, you can see how easily germs are spread and how they can be washed away.

1 Sprinkle a layer of glitter into the tray, and then lightly rub the oil or lotion over your hands.

2 Place your hands in the tray and move them about in the glitter.

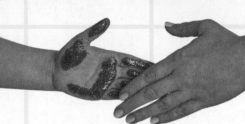

3 Shake your friend's hand. Have you passed on the "germs" to your friend?

4 Pick up a glass. Are there any "germs" left on the glass?

5 Now, wash your hands without soap. How easy is it to remove all the "germs"?

6 Next, wash your hands with soap in warm water for 20 seconds. Rub your hands together and scrub front, back, and between your fingers.

ALL CLEAN!

Scan the **QR code** for step-by-step instructions!

Model Lung

Under your lungs is a muscle called the **diaphragm**. When you breathe in, your diaphragm tightens (or contracts), moving downward. This pulls air into your lungs. When you breathe out, the diaphragm relaxes and moves upward, pushing air out of your lungs.

YOU WILL NEED:

- a plastic bottle
- scissors
- 2 balloons
- a drinking straw
- a rubber band
- modeling clay or sticky tack

1 Ask an adult to carefully cut off the base of the bottle.

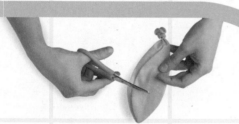

2 Tie a knot in one of the (uninflated) balloons. Cut off the other end.

3 Carefully stretch the balloon over the open bottle base.

4 Push the straw into the other balloon. Wrap a rubber band around the neck to hold it in place. Seal it well, but not so tight that air can't pass through.

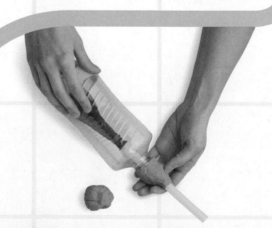

5 Place the straw into the bottle's neck, balloon first. Seal the straw in place using modeling clay.

6 Pull the knotted balloon down. The inner balloon should inflate. The bottom balloon acts like your diaphragm. When it expands, air enters through the straw to fill the space created. The inner balloon inflates, just like your lungs.

... AND BREATHE!

7 Release the knotted balloon. The inner balloon should deflate.

Scan the **QR code** for step-by-step instructions!

It's STEM!

Germs spread easily. To keep them out of experiments, scientists often wear gloves and work in special cabinets with germ-free filtered air.

Soap molecules have two ends: one end mixes with water and the other end sticks to dirt or germs. When you wash, the dirt is bound to the soap and is then washed away with the water.

Many smartphones have **fingerprint** security. They use either light or electrical currents to compare the user's fingerprint with a stored fingerprint in the phone's memory.

Detectives reveal **fingerprints** using a colored powder that sticks to the oils in the fingerprints.

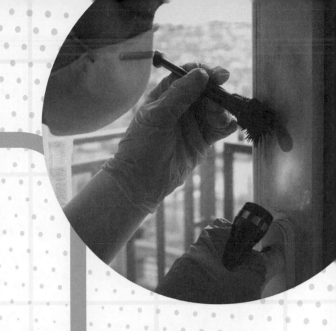

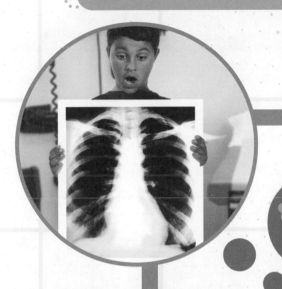

Doctors often use chest X-rays to investigate breathing problems. The **diaphragm** shows up as a thick white layer below the ribs.

You can strengthen your **diaphragm** and feel calmer with belly breathing. Put a hand on your stomach as you slowly breathe in. Your stomach should rise while your chest stays still.

Test Your Nose

The five **senses** are smell, taste, hearing, sight, and touch. They help you perceive the world around you. Smell and taste are closely related. Without a sense of smell, it is much harder to make out different tastes.

1 Pour each drink into a cup.

2 Put on the blindfold.

3 Ask an adult or friend to direct you to one of the cups. Take a sip and guess which liquid you tasted. Repeat for the other four drinks. How many did you get right?

4 Repeat step 3 while holding your nose. How many did you get right this time?

TOP TIP
YOU COULD ALSO USE SOLID FOODS WITH SIMILAR TEXTURES, SUCH AS DIFFERENT FLAVORS OF THE SAME TYPE OF CANDY.

Trick Your Touch

Your skin has millions of touch sensors. Each time you touch something, sensors send a super-fast signal to your brain. When you do this trick, however, your brain is confused. It sees two hands and expects two sensations, but there is only one, and so it doesn't feel anything at all.

YOU WILL NEED:
• an adult or friend

1 Stand facing your friend. Place your right palm against your friend's left palm. Then, watching carefully, stroke your left index finger down the side of both hands as shown in the main photo.

YOUR FINGER WILL FEEL NUMB!

LET YOUR FRIEND TRY THE TRICK. WHAT DOES YOUR FRIEND FEEL?

Growing Mold

Mold is a type of **fungus**. Mold spores are everywhere, but when they land on a food source, such as bread or strawberries, they grow quickly. The mold feeds off the host, breaking down the chemicals inside it. Mold thrives in warm, damp places.

YOU WILL NEED:
- 3 slices of bread
- 3 zipper bags
- water

1 Place one piece of bread in each bag.

2 Sprinkle a small amount of water inside each bag to moisten the bread. Then seal the bags tightly.

3 Place one bag in a sunny window.

4 Place one bag in the refrigerator.

5 Place one bag in a dark cupboard.

6 Check the bags daily to see which one grows the most mold. Why do you think this happened?

WHICH BREAD GROWS MOLD FIRST?

WARNING!
THROW OUT THE SEALED BAGS WHEN YOU HAVE FINISHED THE EXPERIMENT. DON'T TOUCH OR EAT MOLDY FOOD.

YOU COULD ALSO TRY ...

- strawberries
- cheese
- a mix of foods on one plate.

Bean Cycle

Every flowering plant goes through a **life cycle**. It sprouts, grows, produces seeds, and eventually dies. Some of its seeds grow, and the life cycle begins again. Grow some beans to see their life cycle for yourself.

YOU WILL NEED:
- 4 dried lima (butter) beans
- a glass of water
- paper towels or napkins
- a jar
- a pitcher of water
- 4 small pots with soil

1

Place the beans in the glass of water. Leave them to soak overnight.

2

Stuff paper towels or napkins into the jar. Pour in just enough water to wet all the paper.

3

Remove the beans from the water. Push them down the sides of the jar so that you can see them. Place the jar in a warm, dark cupboard.

4

Check the beans every day and add water if the paper is drying out. In a few days, you should see the beans sprout.

5

When you see sprouts, move the jar to a sunny windowsill. Keep watering as needed. You should see roots grow within a couple of weeks.

6 When you see roots, carefully remove the beans. Plant one in the soil of each small pot. Continue to water them and watch them grow.

TAKE PICTURES OF YOUR BEANS EVERY DAY TO SEE HOW THEY CHANGE AND GROW. THIS WILL SHOW YOU THEIR FULL LIFE CYCLE.

Scan the **QR code** for step-by-step instructions!

YOU COULD ALSO TRY ...

... growing an avocado plant from an old avocado pit. Use toothpicks to suspend the dry pit over a glass of water so that it touches the water. Keep it in a warm place and top up the water regularly. Pot the plant in soil once it has grown to about 6 inches (15 cm) tall. Note that avocado plants are much slower to grow than beans, so it could take years to see the full life cycle!

It's STEM!

Professional perfumers strengthen their **sense of smell** by practicing smelling and recognizing different scents.

Toy makers help children learn about their **senses**. This toy introduces young children the feelings of different textures.

The antibiotic penicillin comes from the *Penicillium* **mold**. Here, a microbiologist has grown *Penicillium* in a petri dish filled with nutrient jelly.

Scientists in the Netherlands are working on a biodegradable replacement for plastic made from **fungi**. In the future, chairs and lampshades may be made from a fungus-based fabric.

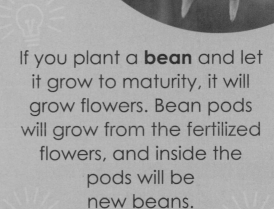

If you plant a **bean** and let it grow to maturity, it will grow flowers. Bean pods will grow from the fertilized flowers, and inside the pods will be new beans.

Farmers around the world grow many different varieties of **legumes**, such as beans, peas, and lentils. Legumes provide protein, which is an important part of a healthy diet.

Celery Colors

A plant soaks up water through its roots. The water travels up the plant, and some of it evaporates from the leaves. This process is called **transpiration**. Adding food coloring to water allows us to see the movement of water through light-colored plants.

1 Fill each glass half full of water.

2 Add several drops of blue food coloring to one glass and several drops of red to the other. Stir it in.

3 Break three stalks of celery from the center of the bunch. Leave the leaves on the top. Ask an adult to slice the ends off neatly.

4 Place one stalk of celery in each glass. Leave the glasses in a warm, sunny place.

5 Check the results after 24 hours.

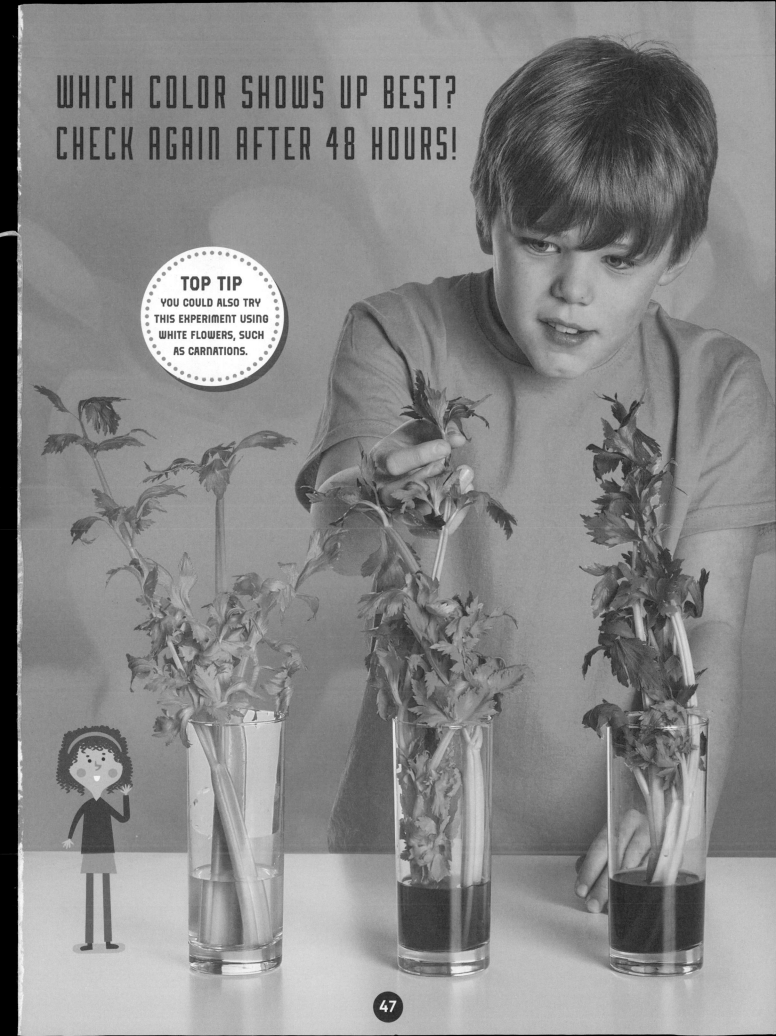

WHICH COLOR SHOWS UP BEST?
CHECK AGAIN AFTER 48 HOURS!

TOP TIP
YOU COULD ALSO TRY THIS EXPERIMENT USING WHITE FLOWERS, SUCH AS CARNATIONS.

Tiny Terrarium

Water falls from clouds as rain. This liquid water then evaporates into water vapor and rises back into the sky. In the cold upper atmosphere, the water vapor condenses into liquid droplets that form new clouds and then fall again as rain. This ongoing process is Earth's water cycle. You can create a mini water cycle in a jar by making this tiny terrarium.

1 Place a layer of pebbles at the bottom of the jar. This gives space for water to drain.

2 Add a thick layer of soil.

3 Plant your plants in the soil. Don't overcrowd them. Leave the top half of the jar empty.

4 Add enough water to moisten the soil, but not so much that there's a pool of water in the pebbles.

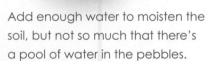

5 Put the lid on the jar, and then place your terrarium in a warm spot, away from direct sunlight.

Scan the **QR code** for step-by-step instructions!

IT'S A WATER CYCLE IN A JAR!

condensation, or "rain"

plant

LET IT LIVE!

The water evaporates in the heat and then condenses to fall as "rain" in your jar.

Add small amounts of water if the soil looks too dry. If it looks too moist, open the lid to let out some water vapor.

Earth Science

Earth science is the study of our planet and its atmosphere. There are different kinds of Earth scientists, including **geologists**, who investigate rocks and minerals, **meteorologists** who study weather and climates, and **oceanographers**, who study the oceans.

Ocean Currents

Cold water sinks, and hot water rises to take its place. In the ocean, this creates a movement of water called a current. Currents move water and floating objects from place to place.

1 Stir 4 drops of blue food coloring into the iced water.

2 Add 6 drops of red food coloring to the hot water. Stir gently.

3 Pour the cold water into the dish until it is about a third full. Use the sieve to remove some of the ice. Add more blue food coloring if needed.

4 Ask an adult to carefully pour hot water into a corner of the dish. Watch the currents swirl!

Swirling Whirlpool

When moving water hits a barrier or meets another current, it rotates around it. If there is a downward force, a powerful funnel, called a **vortex**, is formed. Any objects nearby are sucked down into the vortex.

1

Place the sports-drink cap upside down in the top of one bottle.

2

Tape it in place.

3

Fill the other bottle about three-quarters full with water. Add the food coloring.

4

Screw the empty bottle on top the full one. Tape it tightly in place.

5

Turn the bottles over. Spin the bottles in a circular motion until a vortex forms.

WATCH THE VORTEX SPIN AS THE WATER SWIRLS AROUND THE RISING COLUMN OF AIR.

WOW!

TRY IT WITH BIODEGRADABLE GLITTER INSTEAD OF FOOD COLORING!

Erupting Volcano

Under Earth's crust is a rocky layer known as the mantle. Within the mantle are pockets of molten rock, called magma. Sometimes this magma bursts through the crust in a volcanic eruption. It flows out of the volcano as hot lava and then cools into hard **igneous** rock.

YOU WILL NEED:
- a bottle of soda
- sand (or modeling clay)
- salt
- a funnel
- an outdoor space or tray

1 Place the soda bottle on a flat surface outside or in a tray. Remove the lid.

3 Hold the funnel over the mouth of the bottle.

2 Mold the sand around the bottle so that it looks like a volcano.

4 Carefully but quickly tip salt into the bottle. Then stand back.

STAND BACK!

Scan the **QR code** for step-by-step instructions!

WHEN IT DIES DOWN, TRY ADDING SOME MORE SALT. WHAT HAPPENS THIS TIME?

Soda is supersaturated with **carbon dioxide** gas. When you add salt, the carbon dioxide molecules come out of the solution and stick to the salt grains. Gas bubbles form quickly and rise to the surface.

It's STEM!

Vast amounts of tidal water passing through the Naruto Strait in Japan creates **whirlpools** up to 66 feet (20 meters) wide.

Tornadoes are like whirlpools made from air. They form during storms, when warm, humid air rises up through colder air creating a spinning updraft.

At the Rance Tidal Power Station in France, moving water caused by the **tides** turns 24 turbines, creating **electricity**.

At Whitehaven Beach in Australia, **currents** shift the sand creating shallower and deeper areas. The shallower the water, the lighter its color.

Natural **volcanoes** erupt when molten rock, or magma, under the ground breaks through the Earth's surface becoming red-hot lava. The lava then cools into solid rock.

Scientists who study volcanoes are called **volcanologists**. They have an exciting and sometimes dangerous job.

Rock Types

Rocks form in different ways. **Sedimentary rocks** form when layers of materials such as sand, pebbles, and shells are compacted over time. **Metamorphic rocks** form from extreme heat and pressure inside the Earth. Here, you can make model sedimentary rocks and transform them into metamorphic rocks in your microwave.

YOU WILL NEED:
- 2 clear, microwave-safe containers
- graham crackers
- rice cereal
- chocolate chips
- mini marshmallows
- an oven mitt

1 Break pieces of graham cracker to fit a layer in the base of each container.

2 Sprinkle rice cereal over the top of the cracker in each container.

3 Pour chocolate chips and mini marshmallows and over the cereal.

4 Carefully lay another piece of graham cracker on top. Then repeat this process to create more layers. Gently press down on the top cracker. This forms your layers of sedimentary rock.

5 Microwave one container on medium for 30 seconds and check it. Repeat until the marshmallows and chocolate chips have melted into the other layers. This is your metamorphic rock.

THE LAYERS MERGE!

metamorphic rock

sedimentary rock

Eroding Rocks

Rocks and mountains may seem like they'll last forever, but over many years, wind and water break down the most solid rock. This process is called **erosion**.

1 Use sand and a little water to make four "rocks," each the size of a tennis ball. Put the rocks to one side.

2 Put two rocks in a tray. One is your control. The other is the experimental rock.

WARNING! TO AVOID AN ELECTRIC SHOCK, DO NOT GET WATER NEAR THE HAIR DRYER.

3 Use the hair dryer to blast the experimental rock with "wind" for a few minutes.

4 Use the watering can to simulate rain falling on another rock.

5 Use the hair dryer and then the watering can on a third rock to simulate a storm.

IT'S MONUMENTAL!

AMAZING NATURAL ROCK FORMATIONS DEVELOP WHEN SOME ROCKS ERODE FASTER THAN OTHERS.

RIVER EROSION

You could also try using sand and water to create a model mountain. Trickle water down its side to see how rivers create canyons and valleys.

Scan the **QR code** for step-by-step instructions!

Wind Vane

Wind is moving air. It moves from cooler or drier high-pressure areas to warmer or wetter low-pressure areas. Scientists measure both the speed and direction of the wind. You can measure the wind's direction with a wind vane.

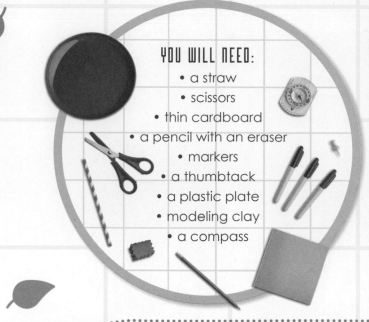

YOU WILL NEED:
- a straw
- scissors
- thin cardboard
- a pencil with an eraser
- markers
- a thumbtack
- a plastic plate
- modeling clay
- a compass

1 Cut two short slits in each end of the straw.

2 Cut an arrow and a tail shape from the cardboard. The tail end needs to be bigger than the arrow. Slide these into the slits on each side of the straw.

3 Cut out a square of cardboard and label the corners N, E, S, and W. Poke the pencil through the center of the square.

4 Push the thumbtack through the straw and into the eraser at the point where the arrow will balance. Push the other end of the pencil into a blob of modeling clay on a plate.

5 Stand up your weather vane and make sure that the arrow will spin freely in the wind. Place the wind vane outside in an open, breezy space. Use a compass to match your N to north.

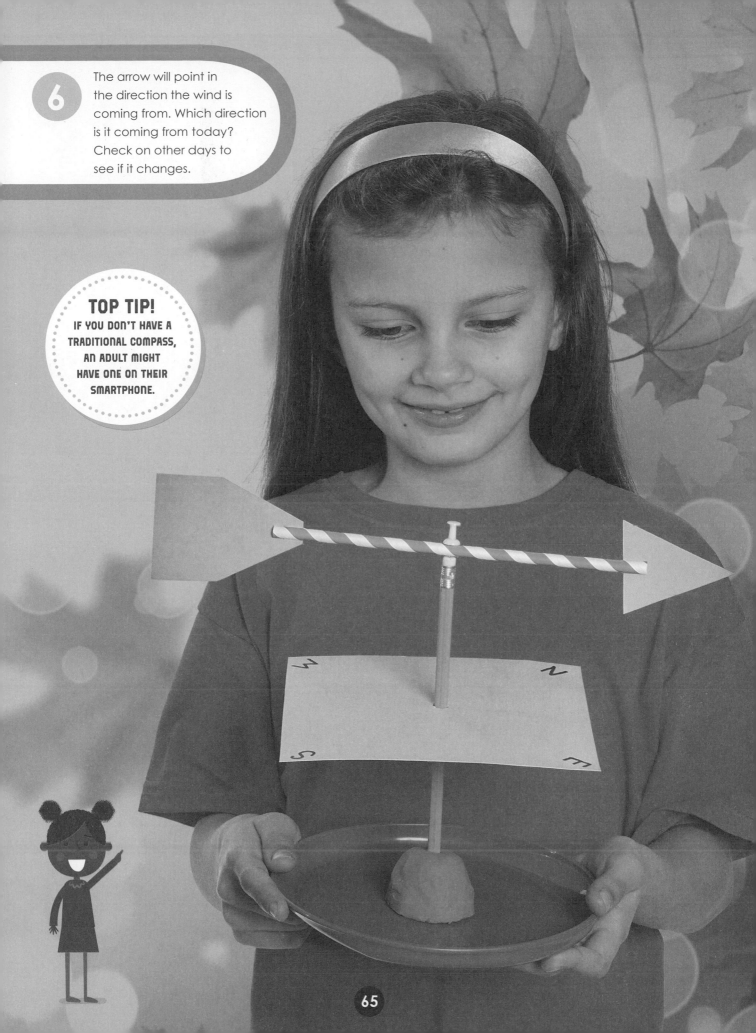

6 The arrow will point in the direction the wind is coming from. Which direction is it coming from today? Check on other days to see if it changes.

TOP TIP!
IF YOU DON'T HAVE A TRADITIONAL COMPASS, AN ADULT MIGHT HAVE ONE ON THEIR SMARTPHONE.

It's STEM!

It is easy to see the layers of **sedimentary rock** in this eroded rock face in Argentina. The rock is soft and crumbly.

Immense heat and pressure under the ground transform sedimentary limestone into smooth, hard **marble**.

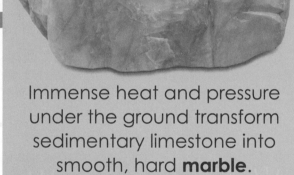

Deep canyons form when river water slowly washes away, or **erodes**, the sediment over millions of years.

Modern **weather stations** allow farmers and scientists to collect data about the wind's speed and direction as well as the temperature, light levels, and humidity.

Many boats have a built-in **compass** so the captain can regularly check the boat's direction. This is important in open ocean, where there aren't landmarks to use for guidance.

When white light enters a glass prism, it splits into the colors that make it up. This is the same process that happens when light passes through raindrops creating a **rainbow**.

Make a Compass

Magnetism is a force. Magnetic objects have north and south poles. Opposite poles pull together and same poles push apart. Inside Earth, electrical currents create a magnetic field. A compass works by magnetizing a needle so it pulls toward to Earth's geographic north.

IF YOU DON'T HAVE A MAGNET, YOU CAN USE THE CLOSURE ON MOST REFRIGERATOR DOORS OR SOME CUPBOARDS.

1 Half fill a bowl with water.

3 Carefully hold the needle at the end and rub the magnet down its length. Repeat this about 20 times. Continue moving in the same direction (down only).

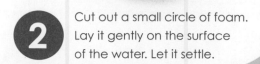

2 Cut out a small circle of foam. Lay it gently on the surface of the water. Let it settle.

4 Gently lay the needle across the foam circle.

IT'S POINTING NORTH!

Scan the **QR code** for step-by-step instructions!

5 Your needle should spin to line up with north. Check it against another compass.

Making Rainbows

White light is made up of all the colors in the rainbow. When sunlight passes through raindrops, each of these colors bends a different amount. This splits them up so we can see them separately.

WARNING!
NEVER LOOK DIRECTLY AT THE SUN. DO NOT LOOK DIRECTLY AT THE SUN'S REFLECTION IN A MIRROR, EITHER.

1 Fill the glass with water.

2 Place the mirror inside at an angle.

3 Place the glass in a sunny spot. Adjust the angle of the mirror until it catches the sun.

LOOK FOR A RAINBOW ON THE OPPOSITE WALL!

IF IT ISN'T SUNNY ENOUGH TO SEE A RAINBOW, TRY TURNING OFF THE LIGHTS AND AIMING A FLASHLIGHT AT THE MIRROR.

Technology

Technology is the use of science to create human-made objects. **Engineers, architects, software developers**, and many other workers create new technologies and improve old ones. Everything from the wheel to the computer was a new technology at some time.

Sound Speakers

Sound travels in waves in all directions outward from its source. Because the sound is spread out, it isn't always all that loud. To make a sound louder, you can collect the sound and point it in a specific direction.

YOU WILL NEED:
- a pencil
- a smartphone with music
- a paper-towel tube
- 2 paper or disposable plastic cups

1 Trace around the bottom of your smartphone (where the speakers are) in the middle of the paper-towel tube.

2 Ask an adult to cut out the shape. They should cut just inside the line for a tight fit.

3 Hold one end of the tube near the base of one cup's side. Trace and cut out just inside the line. Repeat this step for the other cup.

4 Slide the cups onto the ends of the paper-towel tube. Then place your smartphone into the slot, phone speakers down.

PLAY MUSIC!

HOW LOUD?

Play your music without the speakers first. Then, leaving the volume at the same level, play it with your phone in the speakers. How much louder does it sound?

IT SOUNDS LOUDER!

NOW TRY THIS

For a simpler speaker, try placing your phone in a glass cup. The sound collects and travels upward to get out. How does it compare to the tube-and-cup speakers?

Scan the **QR code** for step-by-step instructions!

75

Toothpick Tower

When designing a structure such as a building or bridge, engineers think carefully about the shapes they use. Some shapes are stronger than others. Cubes are an important building block, but they are stronger when reinforced with triangles. Triangles are a strong shape because they don't shear sideways or collapse easily.

YOU WILL NEED:
- toothpicks
- mini marshmallows or gumdrops
- thin cardboard
- crayons
- uncooked spaghetti

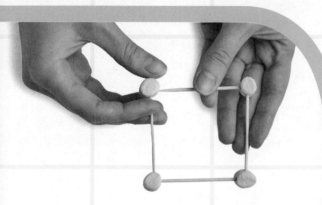

1 Place 4 toothpicks on the table in a square shape. Press mini marshmallows into the corners to create a square.

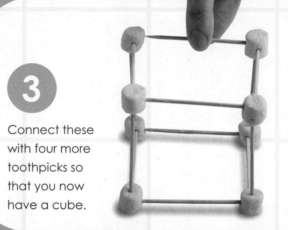

3 Connect these with four more toothpicks so that you now have a cube.

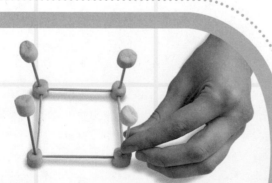

2 Push a toothpick into each marshmallow, sticking straight up. Add a marshmallow on the top of each one.

HOW MANY CRAYONS CAN YOU PILE ON TOP BEFORE THE CUBE STARTS TO COLLAPSE?

4 Place a piece of cardboard across the top.

5

Break spaghetti into pieces long enough to reach across the diagonals of the cube. Press the spaghetti pieces diagonally into the marshmallows on each side of the cube. These are your reinforcements.

HOW MANY CRAYONS CAN YOU PILE ON THIS TIME?

You can build another cube on the first one, using the first cube's top layer as the bottom layer for the new cube. How high can you make your tower?

WITHOUT TRIANGULAR SUPPORTS, A CUBE CAN SHEAR SIDEWAYS LIKE THIS!

Marshmallow Catapult

A catapult is a type of **lever**, which is a simple machine that increases the force you apply. A lever has a long bar that sits across a fixed point called a fulcrum. In a catapult, one end of the bar is fixed. Energy is stored when the lever is pressed down. When it is released, the energy propels the load into the air.

1

Make a stack of 8 Popsicle sticks. Wrap a rubber band around each end to secure them.

2

Make a stack of 2 Popsicle sticks. Secure one end tightly with a rubber band.

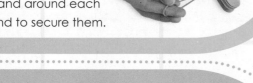

3

Push the larger stack of sticks horizontally between the small stack. Secure it in place with a large rubber band, using an X motion.

4

Lay a spoon along the top stick. Tuck it under the middle and end rubber bands. Wrap another rubber band around its neck to secure it to the stick at the top.

5

Load a marshmallow on the spoon. Hold the base of the catapult with one hand and press down the spoon with your other hand. Then let the spoon go!

6 Make a game by placing bowls in front of the catapult and trying to aim the marshmallows into them.

CAN YOU GET IT INTO A BOWL?

TEST YOUR CREATION

How far can you reach? Try setting targets to hit. Does adding more sticks to the horizontal fulcrum affect the launch?

WARNING!
NEVER AIM YOUR CATAPULT AT A PERSON OR ANIMAL.

It's STEM!

Triangles are strong shapes that can't shear sideways or collapse. This is why they're used in the frames of many bridges, buildings, and towers.

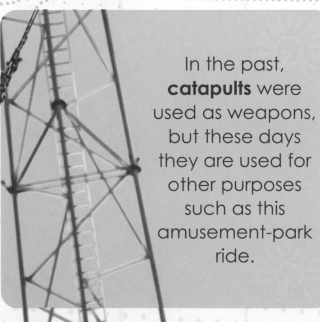

In the past, **catapults** were used as weapons, but these days they are used for other purposes such as this amusement-park ride.

Electronic speakers contain an **amplifier**. This component increases, or amplifies, the strength and volume of the sound using electrical energy.

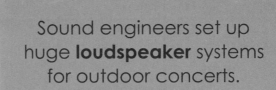

Sound engineers set up huge **loudspeaker** systems for outdoor concerts.

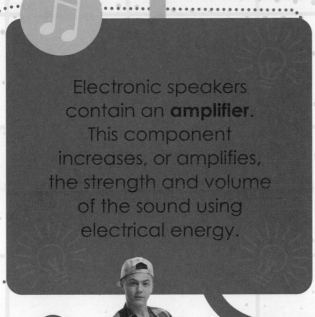

The Eiffel Tower in Paris, France, is an enormous pyramid constructed from four **triangular** sides. Many smaller triangles make up the frame.

Building Bridges

Bridges must be strong enough to hold the loads that cross them. The folds in the second bridge form triangles that spread out the weight of the cars. The two sides of each peak brace each other to help support the load, making it stronger.

YOU WILL NEED:
- 2 cups
- thick paper or very thin cardboard
- scissors
- toy cars

1 Stand the cups upside down, about 6 in (15 cm) apart.

2 Cut out a rectangle of thick paper and lay it across the cups, creating a bridge.

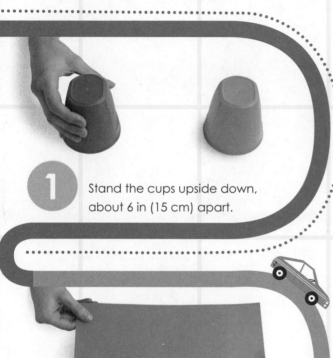

3 Place toy cars in the center of the bridge, one at a time. Count how many you can add before it collapses.

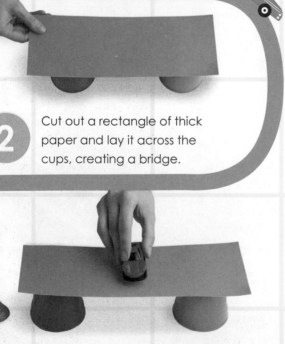

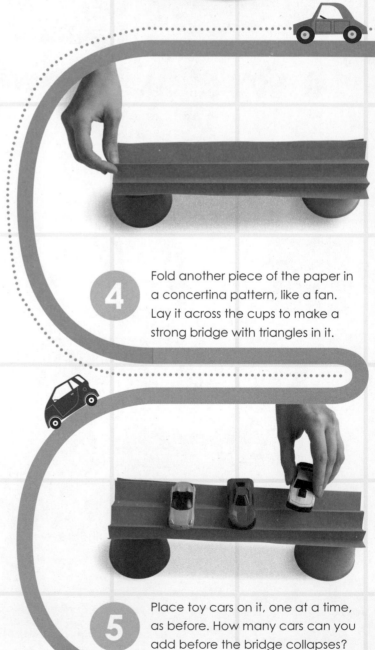

4 Fold another piece of the paper in a concertina pattern, like a fan. Lay it across the cups to make a strong bridge with triangles in it.

5 Place toy cars on it, one at a time, as before. How many cars can you add before the bridge collapses?

Scan the **QR code** for step-by-step instructions!

TRY MAKING BIGGER OR SMALLER FOLDS. HOW DOES THIS AFFECT THE RESULTS?

IS IT STRONGER NOW?

Paddleboat

When an object is stretched or squashed, it gains elastic **potential energy**, or stored energy. When it is released, it uses the energy to spring back to its original shape. You can use this elastic energy to propel a paddleboat forward.

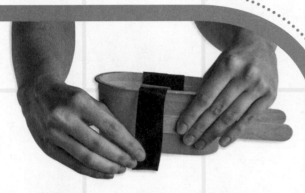

1 Tape a Popsicle stick to each side of the tub so it sticks out halfway behind. Use lots of tape to secure it tightly.

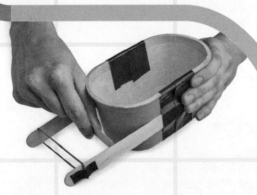

2 Tape the rubber band around the ends of the sticks to connect them. Ask an adult to carefully break a third stick in half and wedge a piece between the other sticks and the tub. It will stop the rubber band pulling the sticks inward.

3 Put the lid back on the boat. Tape the yogurt cup upside down on the lid.

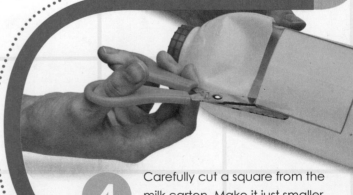

4 Carefully cut a square from the milk carton. Make it just smaller than the distance between your two sticks. This is your paddle.

5 Carefully cut two slits in the paddle.

6 Slide the paddle onto the rubber band, with the center piece over the band and the rest under it. Tape it in place.

7 Place your boat in shallow water. Wind the paddle around as many times as you can, and then let go!

WATCH IT MOVE!

TEST YOUR TUB

Which way does your boat move? Wind the paddle in the other direction. What happens?

Scan the **QR code** for step-by-step instructions!

Floating Hovercraft

When two surfaces touch, a force called friction creates resistance. This slows down a moving object. A hovercraft glides on a thin layer of air between it and the ground. This layer reduces most of the friction, allowing the vehicle to travel quickly and smoothly.

1 Place the sports-drink cap over the hole in the center of the CD. Tape it in place, making sure the seal is airtight. Press the pop-top nozzle down.

2 Blow up the balloon. Hold it tightly at the bottom so that no air comes out, and stretch it over the nozzle until it stands upright. This is your hovercraft.

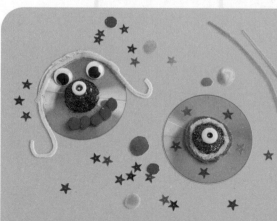

3 Place the hovercraft on a smooth surface, such as a countertop or table. Carefully pull up on the nozzle to release the air. What happens?

You might like to decorate your hovercraft with stickers, pom-poms, and pipe cleaners.

Scan the **QR code** for step-by-step instructions!

WHAT HAPPENS WHEN YOUR HOVERCRAFT RUNS OUT OF AIR? WHY CAN IT NO LONGER HOVER?

TRY YOUR HOVERCRAFT ON DIFFERENT SURFACES. HOW DO THEY AFFECT IT?

It's STEM!

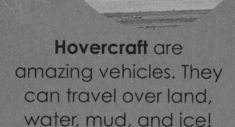

Hovercraft are amazing vehicles. They can travel over land, water, mud, and ice!

Hovercraft are also known as **air-cushion vehicles**, or ACVs. High-pressure air blows under the boat lifting its weight just above the water or ground.

Robotic arms in factories don't always have hands and fingers as we would recognize them.

The latest **prosthetic hands** are controlled by the wearer's brain. Some even allow the person to feel a sense of touch.

In the 1900s, steam engines turned the large paddles on **steamboats**. The boats transported goods and passengers up and down rivers at about 6 miles per hour (10 kph).

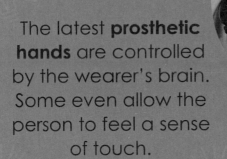

Learning **computer coding** involves breaking a problem into its component parts. It helps build both logical and creative thinking skills, and it's fun!

Robotic Hand

This robotic hand is modeled on your own hand and has joints in the same places. Pulling on the strings has the same effect as contracting muscles: it creates movement.

YOU WILL NEED:
- light cardboard
- a pencil
- scissors
- aluminum foil (optional)
- 5 drinking straws in different colors
- 5 lengths of string or yarn 10 in (25 cm) long
- tape

1 Place your hand on the cardboard and trace around it. Then cut out the shape.

2 Make pencil marks along each of the joints, and fold along the marks. Then cover the hand in aluminum foil.

3 Cut each straw into four different lengths: ¼ in (0.6 cm), ½ in (1.3 cm), 1 in (2.5 cm), and 2 ¼ in (5.5 cm).

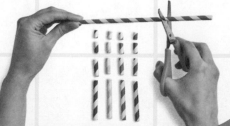

4 Tape the lengths of straw to the hand as shown. The smallest pieces are at the fingertips and the largest on the palm. Shorten any pieces that are too long to fit.

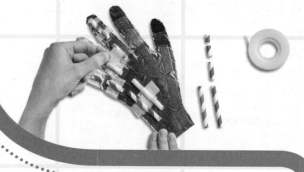

5 Thread a piece of string through the straw on each finger.

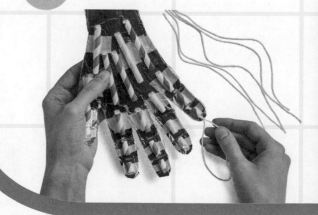

6

Tape each piece of string at the fingertip end. Pull the strings to move the hand.

REAL ROBOTS!

In industry, robotic hands perform tasks that require great strength or great delicacy. They can do the same task over and over without getting tired.

Maze Coding

Computers are programmed using codes. Writing codes involves creating instructions in a precise, step-by-step language. You can practice creating a code by coding a maze for your friends to follow.

YOU WILL NEED:
- a piece of cardboard 8 x 8 in (20 x 20 cm)
- a ruler
- a pencil
- thin cardboard
- scissors
- markers
- a toy
- a friend

1

Using a ruler and a pencil, draw a grid on the cardboard. Make equal sized squares of 1 × 1 in (2.5 × 2.5 cm).

2

Within the grid, design a maze. Use markers to draw walls. Make sure there will be a path from start to finish.

3 On thin cardboard, cut out 27 instruction cards. Make 5 copies of each of these:

Also create 1 card of each of these:

4 On thin cardboard, cut out two small squares 1 in × 1 in (2.5 cm × 2.5 cm). Write "START" on one card and "FINISH" on the other. Place them at the start and finish of the maze.

5 Use your instruction cards to create a code that will lead a friend through the maze, card by card, from the start to the finish.

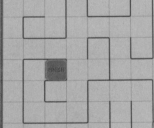

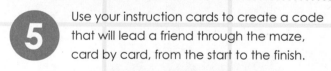

6

Pile up the cards in order, so that the START card will be on top when the pile is turned upside down.

7

Ask a friend to turn over the cards, one by one, and follow the instructions to solve the maze. They can use a small toy as a counter.

START

↑ 3 ■

Glossary

biology   the study of living things, such as plants, animals, and fungi

carbon dioxide   a gas in the air that is made up of carbon and oxygen

chemical reaction   a process in which one or more substances, or chemicals, change into one or more other substances

chemistry   the study of substances, or chemicals, and how they react with one another

concentration   the amount of a substance that is dissolved into a particular amount of liquid

crystal   a solid in which the molecules are linked together in a repeating pattern

diaphragm   a wall of muscle below the lungs that pulls air into the lungs and pushes it out

Earth science   the study of planet Earth and its atmosphere

erosion   the wearing away of rock, soil, and other substances by water, wind, ice, and gravity

freezing point   the temperature at which a liquid freezes. The freezing point of water is 32 °F (0 °C).

fungus   a plantlike living thing that feeds on plant or animal matter. Molds, yeasts, and toadstools are types of fungi.

igneous rock   rock that formed from cooled volcanic lava

lever   a simple machine with a long bar and a pivot point. Levers make work easier. Catapults, wheelbarrows, and seesaws are levers.

life cycle   the changes that a living thing goes through during its life. Childhood and adulthood are stages in the human life cycle.

metamorphic rock   rock that formed underground when its materials were subject to great heat and pressure

meteorology	the study of Earth's atmosphere, climates, and weather
microorganism	a tiny living thing that can only be seen with a microscope. Bacteria and viruses are microorganisms.
non-Newtonian fluid	a liquid that does not behave in the way described by Isaac Newton in the 1600s because its viscosity changes with force, or pressure
oxidization	a chemical reaction in which a substance combines with oxygen. The rusting of metals is an oxidization process.
physics	the study of matter and energy. Physicists study motion, force, electricity, light, sound, and heat.
polymer	a substance made of molecules linked together in long chains of repeating units
potential energy	the energy stored in an object. A stretched rubber band has potential energy. When it is let go, the potential energy will change to movement as it springs back.
sedimentary rock	rock that formed from layers of sediment pressed together by weight
sense	one of the human senses: sight, hearing, touch, smell, or taste
surface tension	a force that causes the top layer of water to act as if it has a skin. Small, light objects can sit on the surface.
technology	the use of scientific knowledge to create and improve things
transpiration	the process in which plants move water from their roots to their leaves, from which some of it evaporates
vortex	a spinning, or spiraling, flow of liquid or gas
water cycle	the constant cycle of Earth's water from evaporation into water vapor, to condensation as droplets in clouds, to precipitation as rain or ice

Index